THE CONCERTO

MOZART, AGED SIX, AT THE COURT OF VIENNA
Oil painting by an unknown artist, 1762.   Mozarteum, Salzburg

JOHN CULSHAW

THE CONCERTO

With 4 Plates in Colour

& 31 Black-and-White

Illustrations

GREENWOOD PRESS, PUBLISHERS
WESTPORT, CONNECTICUT

Library of Congress Cataloging in Publication Data

Culshaw, John.
    The concerto.

    Reprint of the 1949 ed. published by M. Parrish,
London, in association with Chanticleer Press,
New York, which was issued as no. 10 of The World of
music.
    Includes index.
    1. Concerto. I. Title. II. Series: The World
of music (London) ; 10. III. Series: The World of
music (New York) ; 10.
ML1263.C8 1979   785.6   78-60138
ISBN 0-313-20547-7

First published 1949 by Max Parrish and Co. Limited,
London, in association with Chanticleer Press, Inc.,
New York

Reprinted with the permission of Chanticleer Press,
Incorporated

Reprinted in 1979 by Greenwood Press, Inc.
51 Riverside Avenue, Westport, CT 06880

Printed in the United States of America

10 9 8 7 6 5 4 3 2 1

CONTENTS

PLATES IN COLOUR

MOZART, AGED SIX, AT THE COURT OF VIENNA
Oil painting by an unknown artist, 1762
Mozarteum, Salzburg
PAGE 2

A CONCERT PERFORMANCE AT THE BAVARIAN COURT
The Elector Maximilian Joseph III is playing the solo violoncello
Oil painting by Johann Nicolaus Grooth, 1758
Nymphenburg Castle, Munich
PAGE 19

JOSEPH JOACHIM, 1831–1907
Oil painting by G. F. Watts, 1865
Watts Gallery, Compton, Guildford
PAGE 38

IGNACY JAN PADEREWSKI, 1860–1941
Oil painting by Princess Louise, Duchess of Argyll, 1891
Polish Embassy, London
PAGE 55

The colour plates have been reproduced in black and white
in the Greenwood Press reprint edition.

ACKNOWLEDGMENTS

The Editors' thanks are due to the following for the pictures reproduced on the pages mentioned:

COLOUR: frontispiece, Mozarteum, Salzburg; 19, Bayerische Verwaltung der staatlichen Schlösser, Gärten und Seen, Munich; 38, Watts Gallery, Compton, Guildford; 55, the Polish Embassy, London

BLACK-AND-WHITE: 17, the Syndics of the Fitzwilliam Museum, Cambridge; 29, Mozarteum, Salzburg; 34, Universitätsbibliothek, Hamburg; 35, 47, 50 and 63, the Trustees of the British Museum; 56, Messrs. J. & W. Chester Ltd.; 57 and 69, Sir Isaac Pitman & Sons Ltd.; 59, John Rothenstein, Esq., and the Museum and Art Gallery Committee of the Corporation of Birmingham; 61, the Director of the Victoria & Albert Museum; 64, the Proprietors of 'Punch'; 67, Paul Rosenberg Collection, Paris; 71, George Buday, Esq., A.R.E.

ILLUSTRATIONS IN BLACK & WHITE

To
W. E. B.

AUTHOR'S NOTE

Though it cannot aim at being historically complete, this book does attempt to discuss the most important works in the history of concerto form, and to indicate the reasons for their importance. Readers who wish to pursue the subject further are referred to Abraham Veinus's larger book of the same title, and to the third volume of Sir Donald Tovey's 'Essays in Musical Analysis'. I hope also that the latter part of Chapter II in this book may encourage some readers to investigate Professor Girdlestone's admirable volume on 'Mozart's Piano Concertos', at last available in an English translation. I am indebted to Messrs. Boosey & Hawkes for permission to quote the passage from Béla Bartók's Violin Concerto, of which they are the copyright owners.

I

THE DRAMA OF CONTRAST

A brief examination of concert programmes to-day would quickly indicate the popularity of the concerto—from which observation the cynic must not infer that I am writing solely about a certain remarkable work in B flat minor. The apparently insatiable public appetite for works of a particular style is an indication not merely of the popularity of those works, but of a general attitude towards the concerto as a form of music: an attitude which, if taken to extremes, may deprive the listener of considerable musical experiences.

Of one thing we can be quite certain: no single reason will account for this degree of popularity. The weary orchestral player who has blown, banged or sawn his way through fifty performances of a popular concerto in one season will probably tell you that the personality of the soloist, and not the music, is the main attraction; the more aloof variety of critic will explain that the popular type of concerto is one of the easiest and most attractive forms for the listener whose attitude to music is somewhat superficial; the psychologist will study the whole paraphernalia of concerto presentation (including advertising, and the more unorthodox, sub-musical but admittedly spectacular "added attractions" provided by certain soloists), and will tell you that empathy accounts for the more violent examples of public enthusiasm. In each of these explanations there is a certain amount of truth; it is also partially true to say that the presentation in films of either "potted" romantic concertos or specially written works for piano and orchestra, naïvely called concertos and usually qualified by geographical adjectives, has brought many people from the cinema to the concert-hall, avidly in pursuit of the same or similar works deprived of screen action.

Yet it is not too great a generalisation to claim that the concerto is, by nature, a popular form of music. The concerto is a dramatic form, and its real origins, so far as they can be traced, are to be found not so much in instrumental music as in one of the most dramatic of all musical forms—the operatic aria. Such drama is inherent in at least two aspects of the concerto: it is to be found in the element of virtuosity, whether it be the kind required for a revealing performance of Mozart or the very different kind demanded in a brilliant performance of Rachmaninov; it is also present in the element of contrast, which plays so important a part in concerto design—the contrast between the strength of one body of sound and another (volume), and also the contrast between one type of sound and another (tonal distinction). (The derivation of the word "concerto" is a matter that has caused some disagreement. The Italian *concertare*, "to accord together", seems to be the most acceptable source, although a derivation from the Latin *concertare*, "to contend, to debate", is not unreasonable.)

These factors—virtuosity and contrast—can exist together and also independently of one another, and whatever the type of individual application may be, they remain basically dramatic. Thus one may realise that the initial entrance of the solo violin in Elgar's Violin Concerto is intensely dramatic despite the fact that the theme itself is not being introduced for the first time and that, in the opening phrase at least, there is a complete absence of the virtuoso element. The moment is dramatic because its effect is created through the use of the two types of contrast already mentioned.

Another type of drama may be found in such passages as the violent but brief piano cadenzas before the coda of the slow movement of Rachmaninov's Second Piano Concerto. These add nothing to the quality or progress

VIADANA'S 'ECCLESIASTICAL CONCERTOS'
Title-page of collected edition, Frankfort, 1620

of the musical material as such, but are really dramatic interruptions introduced for virtuoso or technical, rather than musical, reasons. From these considerations it follows that the drama in a concerto is not, as some opponents of the form have suggested, a complete reason for assuming that the form is less likely to contain deep musical expression than, for example, a symphony. Such a viewpoint arises, as we shall see, through a concentration on those works whose drama is almost entirely virtuoso by nature—

ORGAN AND ORCHESTRA
Engraving from J. G. Walther's 'Musicalisches Lexicon', 1732

where, in fact, the dramatic element appears to have been added to the music as an afterthought, instead of having been absorbed as an integral quality of the music itself.

Lastly, there is a further dramatic element to be found in the basic conception of the solo concerto as we know it; it is the idea of the individual against the mass—the contrasts, conflicts and possible reconciliations between these two entities. This is not to suggest that any composer has written a concerto specifically to illustrate such a relationship in its human application: it is simply that the musical relationship of the forces in a concerto has been, roughly since the time of Mozart, that of the individual and society. A consideration of this point may help to dispel the regrettably general opinion that a concerto is more or less a symphony with the additional attraction of a soloist. The temptation to adopt such a view with regard to the classical works is perhaps stronger than in the case of the popular romantic concertos, where the disappearance of the orchestral exposition and the early entrance of the soloist seem on their own account to establish a clear distinction. But the concerto has a perfectly respectable history of its own, and has equally an indisputable right to be considered on its own grounds as a musical form, instead of being dismissed (or welcomed) as an inferior (or superior) derivation from the symphony.

A CONCERTO FOR CEMBALO AND CHAMBER ORCHESTRA
Engraving after I. R. Schellenberg. Zurich, 1776

In this book we shall examine the evolution of the concerto by considering those works which would seem to have some claim on the listener's attention, whether by virtue of their popularity or of their historical importance. The latter aspect, which at first sight might seem to be nearer the province of the text-book, is justified by those works which, although enjoying no popularity of their own, have nevertheless influenced others that are very frequently heard.

It is not possible to trace an exact line of evolution for concerto form; the final perfection of the classical conception was the result of not one but a great number of evolutionary factors. The earliest use of the term "concerto" revealed a very broad meaning, and the "concerti ecclesiastici" of Viadana (1564–1645) are as far removed at one extreme from the classical norm as are the concertos of Delius and Schönberg at the other. An examination of sixteenth- and seventeenth-century works bearing the concerto label in some form or other is at first a little dismaying, since one soon finds the term broad enough to cover not only early examples of instrumental music, but also motets, madrigals and even cantatas.

But throughout all these varied applications of the term there exists one commonly recognised quality, without which no work can legitimately be called a concerto: the quality is that of contrast. Thus the motets of Viadana are described as concertos simply because they adopt the procedure—unusual for their period—of adding an organ accompaniment to the choir part, thereby achieving a degree of contrast. In its elementary basis, therefore, the term concerto can be said to cover those pieces where two or more instruments (or groups of instruments, or voices) are so blended that they display both the concerted and individual possibilities of the instruments. Even before the Viadana motets it is possible to find works which, if not actually bearing the title "concerto", are nevertheless early examples of the concerto principle: one such example, still occasionally to be heard, is Gabrieli's "Sonata piano e forte" (1597) in which tonal contrast is achieved by the use of two instrumental groups, one consisting of high brass instruments and the other of low brass and strings.

Nevertheless, it is clear that an exhaustive pursuit of concerto origins would lead to the unknown primitive who first thought of any type of musical sound combination and tonal contrast, and therefore it is true to say that the basis of the concerto is among the fundamentals of music. It is not until much later that we come across the very definite division between the concerto and the symphony, although obviously the principle of tonal contrast applies to some extent in all forms of music. But whereas it was

HEINRICH SCHÜTZ IN THE LAST YEAR OF HIS LIFE
Engraving by Christian Romstedt, 1672

absorbed into the general requirements for a symphony and became no more than one of many such essentials, in the case of the concerto it assumed from the earliest times a position of the utmost importance. And as late as 1943 Bartók called one of his last orchestral compositions a *Concerto for Orchestra* simply because the general design of the work encouraged the most vivid contrasts between varied orchestral groups and therefore, in the broad sense, qualified the work for its title.

In 1636 there appeared the *Kleine geistliche Konzerte* (Little Sacred Concertos) by Schütz which, although still classifiable as motets, seemed to foreshadow the same composer's later use, in oratorio, of more adventurous tonal contrasts; the influence in this case may have come from Monteverdi, whose frequent use of a single voice in alternation with an instrumental group is not greatly different from the concerto principle.

It was approximately at the period when instrumental music began to usurp the autocracy of the voice that the concerto began to flourish in a more precisely definable form. With the development of small orchestras, and also instrumental groups no longer restricted to the mere accompaniment of voices, it was not surprising that certain instruments should be favoured by certain composers, nor that players should have discovered that technical agility is not the sole prerogative of the vocalist. The concerto principle can therefore be recognised in many early orchestral compositions through the appearance of individual instruments or groups serving the functions of a solo; where this solo is truly individual, in the sense that it is played by one musician, it is possible to recognise the beginnings of the solo instrumental concerto as we know it.

The emergence of the solo applied not only to orchestral works, but also to forms of chamber music; in the first half of the seventeenth century Valentini wrote a work for violin, bassoon, cornettino and trombone in which each instrument has a separate movement in which to appear as soloist; similarly Dario Castello uses the words "Sonata concertante" to describe a work for violin and bassoon, written during the same period. But it is not until the end of the seventeenth century that we can recognise a more definite usage of the term concerto, and this was its application to the form known as the concerto grosso.

The establishment of the concerto grosso was largely due to the compositions in that form by Alessandro Scarlatti, Torelli and Corelli; in particular, it was the compositions of the last-named composer that appeared to act as a model for the future. Corelli's opus 6 consists of a set of twelve concertos, designated as such because of the implicit contrast between two musical groups, one of which is larger than the other. Imagining a string orchestra as the basis, one can think of the division of this orchestra into two groups, the larger called the *concerto grosso*, or *ripieno*, and the smaller called the *concertino*. Of course, such a division may exist in the case of works that are not generally regarded as concertos; by the smallest extension of the concerto-grosso principle it would be legitimate, for instance, to classify Elgar's *Introduction and Allegro for Strings* as such, since the work employs

GEORGE FREDERICK HANDEL
Oil painting by Giuseppe Grisoni

the forces of string orchestra and string quartet. This point is mentioned because it is necessary to remember that, despite the example of Corelli's charming works, there had yet to evolve a distinctive form, rather than a distinctive principle, for the concerto.

The works of Corelli served as the models for concerto compositions by Geminiani, Locatelli, Vivaldi and others. Approximately four hundred concertos are attributed to Vivaldi, although the authenticity of half this number has been questioned. And although his works are structurally in some ways more interesting than those of Handel, it is nevertheless the latter's concertos that are heard the more frequently to-day. Handel's contribution to the evolution of the concerto can be seen from two aspects of his work: there is the introduction (in the set of opus 3) of wind instruments, and there is the immediately apparent breadth of variety in expression in the forms and styles of the various movements. In Handel's treatment the relationship between *ripieno* and *concertino* seems, according to the angle from which one chooses to view it, either to broaden or restrict the use of the individual, as distinct from the grouped, solo. Thus it is possible to find movements in Handel's concerti grossi that are truly in the nature of the solo concerto; an example is to found in the movement for violin and orchestra in no. 6 of opus 6. On the other hand, he liked to alter the balance of his forces from movement to movement, thereby preventing the domination of the work by any one soloist, and at the same time ensuring a wide range of instrumental variety.

We have not, so far, paid special attention to the relation between the concerto and the vocal aria, although it is general knowledge that the cadenza in a concerto is by origin a vocal rather than instrumental device. But whereas cadenzas are usually little more than appendages to the form of the solo concerto, there exists in fact a far more important bond between the aria and the concerto. If we consider the arias of Alessandro Scarlatti, or many of those by Handel, we can immediately recognise an underlying principle of contrast between the solo voice and orchestra; beyond that, it is clear that since these arias are not unorganised rhapsodies they must be constructed on a basis that is capable of combining dramatic contrast with a balanced and musically coherent form. Thus, to take a simplified example, we may imagine an aria in which the orchestra first presents a theme which, at its conclusion, is taken up by the singer, the orchestra then retiring into the background. The importance of this apparently simple device has been pointed out by Sir Donald Tovey in his essay *The Classical Concerto*, in which he remarks that "this arrangement brings out the force of the solo in thrusting the orchestra into the background, while at the same time the orchestra has had its say and need not seem unnaturally repressed . . . as it would seem if it were employed only to support the solo".

Equally in the original relation between voice and orchestra in the aria, it is not difficult to detect further features applicable to the concerto; one has only to think of the element of repetition, or of the way in which a solo phrase or statement will be gently underlined by the accompaniment until the climax is reached, at which point the relatively feeble power of the solo voice or instrument will require greater support to prevent the danger of anticlimax. Indeed, for examples of these specific points it is not even necessary to turn to the classical or pre-classical concertos; Tchaikovsky's famous Violin Concerto shows, particularly in the first movement, the composer's realisation that a soloist needs support at a climax (even of the

A CONCERT PERFORMANCE AT THE BAVARIAN COURT
The Elector Maximilian Joseph III is playing the solo violoncello
Oil painting by Johann Nicolaus Grooth, 1758. Nymphenburg Castle, Munich

lyrical variety), and it is interesting to study the way in which he achieves this support and yet avoids the pitfall of swamping the solo part, which might create an even worse kind of anticlimax.

The fact that J. S. Bach was fully aware of the relation between certain vocal forms and the concerto is not only evident in the formal aspects of his works but is clearly illustrated by the way in which he transformed a movement from his First Brandenburg Concerto into a secular cantata, *Vereinigte Zwietracht der wechselnden Saiten*; the bond is further indicated by the evidence that the transformation consists of an expansion of a single violin solo (in the original) into a four-part chorus (in the cantata).

Bach's most important contribution to the concerto repertoire is the set of six Brandenburg Concertos, so called because of their dedication to the Margrave of Brandenburg. They remain, in almost unanimous estimation, the highest achievements in concerto-grosso style, and they encompass a range of expression and a command of instrumental colour unknown before their time. The exquisite and brilliant second concerto of the set is scored for trumpet, oboe, flute and violin (as *concertino*) with accompanying *ripieno* for strings, while the fifth has violin, flute and cembalo soloists—the cembalo making its first appearance as a solo instrument, complete with elaborate cadenza. Numbers three and six of the Brandenburg set are no less interesting than the others, despite the absence of colourful solo instruments, and their superficial similarity to the older models of Corelli. So slight is this similarity, and so disarming is the music, that one may on occasion be tempted to forget that the Third Brandenburg work, for instance, is a concerto at all. In Bach's hands the division of the string orchestra ceases to be simply a matter of *concertino* and *ripieno*; instead it becomes a far more pliable medium, maintaining its concerto basis by alternations between an orchestra playing in three parts, and the same orchestra divided into nine. And throughout the Third Brandenburg Concerto, as in the others, it is always possible to trace the fundamentals that became apparent when we considered the aria. The interplay of solo and orchestra presents the musical material in its most varied and attractive form. The material is then extended; there are passages for the soloists without accompaniment, and further ritornelli to remind the soloists not to stray too far from the argument; there are also gradual progressions to a climax, and a fusion at that point of the two contrasted groups. These are qualities that are common to the elementary aria form and to Bach's Brandenburg Concertos. They are qualities that we shall find to be equally applicable, although in a modified way, to the classical concerto.

II

THE ENTRY OF THE SOLOIST

A LTHOUGH it is possible to trace a long evolutionary line for the solo concerto, and although that line does not uniformly follow that of the concerto grosso, it will be sufficient for our purpose if we concentrate on the concertos of Bach, Handel and Mozart and pay only small attention to their forerunners. Yet there are two particular aspects of the solo concerto that cannot be applied, as generalisations, to the concerto grosso. The first is obvious, and is simply the problem of balance between an *individual* solo and orchestra. The second is a rider which marks an important difference between the two mediums. It is the fact that polyphonic treatment of material—so evident in the concerto grosso—is not nearly so important a feature of the solo concerto, simply because the uneven forces in the work are less capable of achieving a complex interweaving of sound in the musical texture. This is, of course, not to be taken as a denial of the existence of fugal treatment in concertos, since there are plenty of striking examples; such passages exist, for instance, in the last movements of Beethoven's Third, Brahms's First and Rachmaninov's Second Concertos, yet in all such cases it is the orchestra that carries the weight of the fugue, which is usually written not for its own sake but in order to present the soloist with the opportunity to make an effective entry, thereby appearing in contrast with the complex texture of the fugue. This, in fact, is precisely what happens in the case of the first two works I have just quoted; in the case of Rachmaninov, the piano takes part in the fugue for a matter of seconds, after which the treatment is abandoned.

Vivaldi, whose works in concerto-grosso form have already been mentioned, wrote a large number of violin concertos which combine charming music with a necessary element of showmanship. These works enjoyed a considerable popularity in their time, and some of them were later transcribed by Bach for performance on the clavier. ("Clavier" is a word used to denote a keyboard instrument. According to period, it may be applied to the harpsichord, clavichord or pianoforte.) It is significant that during this period the solo cadenza emerged as an essential part of concerto form, coming in towards the end of the first movement where, generally, it remained until Mendelssohn thought of a new—and indeed superior—position.

It is evident that Vivaldi used his violin concertos not only as pieces for concert performance, but also as teaching material for his pupils; equally, throughout this period, there can be traced hundreds of concertos written by musicians whose primary interest lay in teaching rather than in composition. Such works are of little musical value to-day, although they are interesting because they can show us some of the technical problems of the period. But in the case of Vivaldi, who was a real composer, one finds that the purely technical aspect is always secondary to that of musical expression.

The potentialities of the clavier as the solo instrument in a concerto was a matter of great interest to Bach; the experiment already mentioned in the Fifth Brandenburg Concerto led him to adapt, or transcribe, a number of works into the form of concertos for clavier and orchestra. A great deal of research has been carried out in order to determine the originals of these transcriptions, and also to suggest reasons why Bach, although clearly fond of the clavier as a solo instrument, did not choose to write original works in the form. The reasons are numerous and complex, but in general it may be said that in his clavier concertos Bach was acting as an empiricist; he was very possibly more interested in the potentialities of the form than in the actual music he might convey through that form. We know that three of the seven clavier concertos are transcriptions of the violin concertos in A minor, E major and D minor (the latter for two violins), and it is possible that some of the other clavier concertos are also arrangements of works for the violin, the originals of which have not been found; similarly, the sixth concerto is a transcription of the Fourth Brandenburg, the flutes being retained as part of the accompanying body and the violin being replaced by the clavier. It is also evident that the concerto for four claviers and orchestra is a transcription of a concerto for four violins by Vivaldi, whilst all four organ concertos are known to be arrangements of works by Prince Johann Ernst and Vivaldi.

On this basis, some might assume that Bach's contribution to the field of concertos (apart from the violin works and the Brandenburgs) consisted of little more than clever "hack" work, with the single praiseworthy quality of preserving for posterity a quantity of music by other composers which might otherwise have been forgotten. But whilst it may be admitted that Bach's finest music will not be found in the clavier concertos, it should be remembered that had it not been for the attention he gave to the form through the medium of transcription, the position of Mozart—and indeed the whole history of the classical concerto—might have been very different. In Bach's clavier concertos the relationship between soloist and orchestra

JOHANN SEBASTIAN BACH
Lithograph, 1858; probably after a painting by E. G. Haussmann

is not clearly defined; there are movements in which the orchestra is silent throughout, and there are also movements in which the solo part proceeds in such close union with the accompaniment that the title of concerto seems hardly justified. Yet beyond any doubt Bach's experiments indicated the powers of the clavier (and hence the piano) as the solo instrument most capable of retaining its individuality when supported by an accompanying body of strings.

Before approaching the group of works which collectively constitute the highest pinnacle in the solo-concerto range—Mozart's piano concertos —it is necessary to survey very briefly the organ concertos of Handel, and the works written in concerto form by Haydn. Handel's organ concertos, of which there are four volumes, are brilliant virtuoso works which are

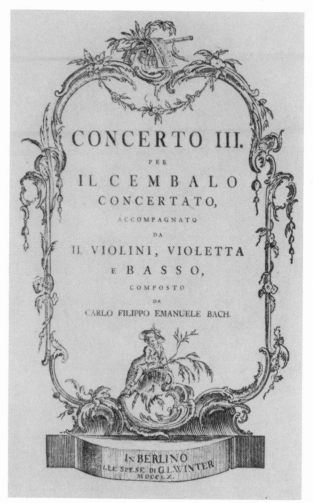

CARL PHILIPP EMANUEL BACH'S THIRD CEMBALO CONCERTO
Engraved title-page

decidedly more interesting than the similar works by Bach. As one would expect from a composer whose prime interest was the stage, they are powerfully dramatic compositions, and Handel clearly understood the opportunities presented by a combination of organ and orchestra. Yet there is something strangely unsatisfactory about all organ concertos, and the reason

JOHANN CHRISTIAN BACH
Engraving by F. Bartolozzi after A. Carlini, 1791

for this is probably the difficulty of blending organ and orchestra without one dominating the other, plus the rather weak contrast that is obtained when the two forces act in dialogue. But these observations are retrospective; Handel's concertos were extremely popular in their time, and their popularity was partly due to the composer's outstanding abilities as an organist.

The period between the concertos of J. S. Bach and those of Mozart is marked by a number of further developments in the style and form of the clavier concerto, conspicuously evident in the works of Carl Philipp Emanuel and Johann Christian Bach. But before the classical concerto could at last emerge, it was necessary that the classical sonata form should first be established as a medium for musical expression, and this establishment came to fruition largely through the symphonies, quartets and sonatas of Haydn. Haydn's concertos, on the other hand, can hardly be classed as milestones in the history of the form, although the development of the orchestra enabled him to be more adventurous than any members of the Bach family in the scoring of his solo concertos; the enrichment of the orchestra by the addition of wood-wind to the body of strings was a development which, in Mozart's hands, led to the establishment of the former as a group no less important than the latter. One has only to hear the slow movement of Mozart's C minor Piano Concerto (K. 491) to realise how important a part the wood-wind is capable of taking.

Haydn also employed, on occasions, a more vivacious style of keyboard writing than that of J. C. Bach, and the fact that only two of his twenty piano concertos have survived is due more to the competition of Mozart than to any intrinsic defects in the music. His nine violin concertos have suffered a similar fate, and while one of his six 'cello concertos (the work in D major) has managed to maintain its position in the repertoire, its composition has for many years been mistakenly attributed to Anton Kraft, a pupil of Haydn; recent research has shown, however, that beyond any doubt the work is Haydn's own. It does not become any the more important through this discovery, although its audience may now be increased by the addition of those who previously adopted a somewhat condescending attitude to what they believed to be the work of a lesser composer.

It is only when we reach the period of Mozart's piano concertos that we can recognise a state of maturity in the concerto form, amounting to a position of independent importance and requiring no comparisons with symphonies, operas or sonatas. If we wish to understand the extent of Mozart's achievement, and its effect on the concertos of the future, it is necessary at once to abandon any preconceived ideas about the rigidity of classical concerto form. It is far preferable to examine Mozart's earlier works through our knowledge of the vocal aria and the concerto grosso than to endeavour to align them with some blue-print of classicism. In the first place we can recognise a parallel between the orchestral ritornello (or introduction) as it appears in the aria and as it appears in the concerto; its purpose

JOSEPH HAYDN
Lithograph after a drawing by George Dance, 1794

in both cases is to introduce the musical material and to prepare for the entry of the soloist, although obviously the ritornello in a concerto is likely to be larger and longer than in the case of an aria. Contrary to the recipe prescribed by most programme notes, the ritornello does not necessarily introduce all the material, and frequently in the case of Mozart the identity of the so-called "second subject" is by no means established until its importance has been stressed *by the solo instrument.* When the soloist enters, there exists no certain rule by which we can tell exactly which themes are to be selected for development; the piano, in all probability, will make its entry on material not previously heard, although in some cases (the Concerto in A major, K. 488, for instance) it may concentrate on a repetition, with embroideries, of themes already stated in the orchestral ritornello.

An analysis of any of the mature Mozart concertos reveals the presence of intellect as well as emotion, and the balance between these factors is frequently very delicate. The important thing to remember when listening to the first movement of any Mozart concerto is that the music was written in a certain form because that form, in all but its broadest outlines, was dictated by the material, and not by any conception of "pure classicism", whatever that may be. For that reason I shall not attempt to examine any single Mozart concerto in detail, since to do so would only indicate the construction of that work. And since listening to music—and Mozart in particular—is not simply a matter of understanding construction, we shall in this book avoid any conventional analysis of his works.

When Mozart began to compose, the solo concerto was a relatively young form; at first, therefore, he concentrated on transcriptions of works by other composers—notably J. C. Bach—and it was not until he was seventeen that he wrote his first wholly original concerto. During the course of his short life he composed twenty-one piano concertos (not including those for two or three pianos and orchestra), and there would undoubtedly have been more if Mozart had been given more opportunities to play his works, since his concertos were written specifically for his own performance.

The common fallacy that Mozart's concertos are alike in construction leads to an even more pernicious belief which postulates that, although "pretty" and "classically" perfect, Mozart's concertos are not very deep—they consist, it is alleged, of music of such purity that real emotional expression is denied to them. This particularly nonsensical viewpoint arises, one suspects, because Mozart's works do not happen to express the same emotions as the concertos of Tchaikovsky, and because subtlety of expression is an elusive quality that may not be immediately appreciated by those who prefer music that wears its heart on its sleeve. In Mozart, simplicity and profundity are inextricably bound together; the listener who notices only the former may or may not eventually discover the latter. Certainly no one but Mozart can convince him that such a quality exists.

A study of Mozart's mature concertos soon reveals a single quality—that of emotional expression—which dominates all other factors in the music, including the form. Why, in the A major Concerto (K. 488), does Mozart write a *tutti* full of material, permit the soloist to repeat virtually all that material, and then proceed to introduce a completely new melody on which the development of the movement is entirely based? Why, in his C minor Concerto (K. 491), does he suddenly decide that the piano shall take part in the coda of the first movement? Similar questions could be posed about certain features in all the concertos, but these features only become irregularities if one persists in regarding Mozart as a cold classicist, tied to some

MOZART WITH HIS FATHER AND SISTER
The portrait of his mother hangs on the wall
Oil painting done by an unknown artist at Salzburg, 1780 or 1781

system of formal construction that is more mathematical than musical. It is only when these features are examined in relation to the movements of which they are part that they are seen to be anything but mathematical.

Similarly, the "emancipation" of the orchestra is often said to be Beethoven's prerogative. Yet this is a generalisation that may only be defended by ignoring Mozart's concertos in E flat, C minor, A major or D minor, to mention only four. The richness of the wood-wind writing in the slow movement and finale of the C minor work has virtually no parallel in concerto history, either before or since its time. It is true that Beethoven uses a larger orchestra than Mozart, and that its part is more powerful; to say this, however, is not to claim that its part is any more important than that of the orchestra in Mozart's concertos. But it should also be remembered that the apparent thinness of the solo part in many of Mozart's exquisite slow movements is due to the fact that such parts were written only as

THE LÖCHELPLATZ AT SALZBURG
Mozart was born in the left-hand house at the end of the square
Lithograph by C. Czichna after I. A. Wenzl

outlines, with the intention that the ornamentation should be added by the soloist at the performance.

In the same way, the cadenza in the first movement is an essential part of the Mozart concerto, and here again the intention was that the soloist should improvise. We can be thankful that Mozart provided cadenzas for a number of his concertos; other composers have since attempted to write cadenzas for those works lacking an authentic specimen, but with very few exceptions the results have proved stylistically and emotionally incompatible with their context.

Between 1784 and 1786 Mozart wrote twelve piano concertos, an act of intensive creation prompted by the acclaim with which he had been received as a pianist in Vienna. But the composition of twelve major works in so short a time would not be remarkable were the quality not so high; these works comprise Mozart's finest essays in concerto form, and the range of emotion contained in them is extraordinary. Likewise, Mozart clothes his ideas in whatever type of form is most applicable to their character. Thus a slow movement may be simply an imaginative treatment of two or three themes (K. 488), a rondo (K. 491) or possibly a set of variations (the two B flat concertos, K. 450 and K. 456); and although Mozart's finales are usually in rondo form, they can on occasions be something different—as in the case of the C minor Concerto (K. 491), which uses a theme and variations for its finale. This particular concerto seems in many ways to be the finest of the set. It is an extraordinary work, the importance of which in concerto history may easily be underestimated. (Beethoven's Third Concerto in C minor and Brahms's First in D minor each owe something to the example of K. 491.) Its orchestration is unusually rich, even for Mozart, and the emotional intensity of its music is indescribable in words. Only the music itself can explain the reason for the breathless, hushed conclusion of the first movement, which seems in a way to anticipate the somewhat ghostly march that appears as the variation theme in the finale. Between these movements is a Larghetto of such disarming simplicity that the best one can do to convey something of its beauty is to quote the concluding bars. Those who wish to ask questions about the nature of inspiration in musical composition should examine the accented passing notes marked "x" in the example, for at that moment they may recognise the working of a great imagination:

Mozart's death at the age of 36 was a tragedy to be deplored, but in his case there is no need to add the pious observation: "If only he had lived a little longer he might . . ." In his piano concertos Mozart left a legacy of music that has still to be explored by all but a few specialists. I have not mentioned his concertos for violin, bassoon, clarinet or for combinations of more than one instrument; these works contain magnificent music, but even so it is to the piano concertos that we must turn to find the essence of Mozart's expression in concerto form. In his book on Mozart, Alfred Einstein said: "Listeners who can really appreciate Mozart's piano concertos are the best audience there is." Such an opinion arises from a deep knowledge of the music, rather than from an observation of audiences. To understand Mozart, however, is not to deny oneself the pleasure of the noisier, more exciting romantics. It is to add to one's store of musical knowledge, and it is an addition that no other music on earth can provide.

III

THE MUSIC COMMANDS THE FORM

THE seven works in concerto form by Ludwig van Beethoven mark the transition from the style of the "classical" composers to the new age of romanticism. The differences between the two are hard to define, since the transition was gradual and was assisted by widely different influences, not the least of which was the expansion of the orchestra, together with the improved technique of orchestral musicians. It is wiser, therefore, not to regard the two periods as opposite poles, but to consider romanticism as the offspring of nineteenth-century thought applied to established musical principles. Such an application is nowhere more clearly reflected than in Beethoven.

Sometimes one hears it said that Beethoven's First and Second Piano Concertos (the so-called Second, in B flat, is the first in order of composition) are so heavily indebted to Haydn and Mozart that they can only be regarded as experiments in the form; there is some truth in this, since it is obvious that Beethoven was by no means unaware of Haydn or Mozart, or Clementi for that matter. Nevertheless, the individuality of Beethoven is clearly discernible in both works; despite the Haydn-like joviality of the finale of the C major Concerto, the tantalising rhythmic construction of its first theme could only have come from Beethoven, and pianists still seem to have some difficulty in deciding where to place the strong accents:

Another difference between Beethoven's early concertos and those of his predecessors is the relatively thicker style of the piano writing. The solo part is always written out in full, so that none of his scores has the apparent

LUDWIG VAN BEETHOVEN
Engraving after Louis Letronne, 1815

austerity of some of Mozart's slow movements; also, Beethoven realised that *concertante* passages for the soloist were in imminent danger of becoming stereotyped. He avoided such clichés by devising new figurations and writing a more active and brilliant left-hand part in those passages where the piano was required merely to accompany an important statement by the orchestra. All these points of style indicate that his early piano concertos are much more than imitations of an already perfect original.

Beethoven's real experiments began with the Third Concerto, in C minor, op. 37. This work precedes the Second Symphony, and was written at a particularly crucial period of Beethoven's life, for between 1798 and 1800 he first realised that the approach of deafness was no longer to be regarded as a temporary disability but as an inevitable and unavoidable permanency. This he must have known when writing the Third Concerto, and in 1806, the year of the Fourth Concerto, he was not only reconciled to the

BEETHOVEN'S 'HEILIGENSTADT TESTAMENT'
Part of the third page, and signature with seal

approaching silence, but was busily composing some of his finest music.
Beethoven's fortitude in the face of a musician's most dreaded affliction
becomes even more remarkable when we consider the *kind* of music he was
able to write during the worst years of trial—the years during which deafness gradually became more acute. The intensity of his suffering is indicated
by the so-called "Heiligenstadt Testament", addressed to his brothers and
written in 1802, from which the following is a quotation:

> ... that beloved hope, which I brought with me when I came here, to be
> cured at least in a degree, I must wholly abandon—as the leaves of autumn fall
> and are withered, so hope has been blighted ... O Providence, grant me at
> last one day of pure joy—it is so long since real joy echoed in my heart ...

Yet the tragedy of these words finds no reflection in the music he composed
during the period; to realise this, one has only to consider the Second
Symphony, or the Third, Fourth and Fifth Piano Concertos—the last of
which was written in 1809, one year after he had made his final appearance

BEETHOVEN'S CADENZA FOR MOZART'S PIANO CONCERTO IN D MINOR (K. 466)
From the autograph score at the British Museum

in public as a virtuoso pianist. The way in which Beethoven's music transcended the personal tragedy of his deafness in order to dwell on deeper, universal expression is an aspect of his genius which may serve to remind us that it is not always wise to expect a composer's life to be reflected in his music.

Some knowledge of Beethoven's personality is, however, a useful background to a study of the concertos, since those works are no less characteristic (though emotionally more restricted) than the symphonies. It is in the Third, in C minor, that Beethoven faced his particular problems in the concerto form. As we have seen, the growth of the symphony governed, to some extent, the evolution of at least the first movement of the solo concerto, and Beethoven's C minor work suggests a certain degree of tension between the two forms. The whole structure of the long orchestral exposition seems to indicate conflicting desires, one of which tends to follow the design of the Mozartian ritornello while the other seeks to broaden this outline so that it becomes more specifically symphonic in character. The danger here is obvious: if the orchestral introduction is of large dimensions it may well arouse such interest on its own account that the entry of the soloist may seem to be an anticlimax, or an unnecessary diversion. And since the concerto had clearly become a form suitable for symphonic musical thought, Beethoven's problem was immediate and unavoidable.

A complete account of his solution would demand a lengthy analysis, but the matter can be summarised by considering three "innovations", one being wholly original and two having clear precedents. In his Fourth and Fifth Concertos Beethoven allowed the soloist to enter *before* the orchestral exposition, although the latter remained an essential part of the general design. The entrance of the soloist before the orchestra (in the Fourth Concerto) and in dialogue with the orchestra (in the Fifth Concerto) does not therefore alter the function of the ritornello, but merely establishes the nature of the work. (It is interesting to note that in Mozart's E flat Concerto (K. 271) the soloist enters at the second bar of the exposition, an experiment which may have been in Beethoven's mind when he was drafting his Fourth Concerto.) The initial entry of the soloist in Beethoven's Fourth Concerto leads to an even more startling innovation, which is the immediate entry of the orchestra *in the wrong key*—B major instead of G major. By this principle Beethoven increased the scope of the orchestral exposition by writing themes that frequently pass through a number of keys—amounting to a matter of hint or suggestion rather than emphatic modulation. Furthermore, as if to compensate for this broadening of the exposition, he merged the conclusion of the *tutti* with the entry of the soloist, thereby achieving fluency and continuity. In this way the most powerful and organised of expositions is prevented from being anything more than a prolonged anticipation of the soloist's second entry.

But Beethoven knew that these formal innovations were only of value if they were flexible enough to vary with the character of his themes; the music must still command the form. Thus the soloist opens the Fourth Concerto by playing the main theme, but at the opening of the "Emperor" (Fifth) the solo part consists of arpeggios and flourishes, the orchestra having the first statement of the themes. This difference of treatment is not a matter of whim, but a question of musical necessity. The opening theme of the Fourth Concerto is simple, quiet, and of more harmonic than melodic interest; it is eminently suitable for introduction by the piano. But the main theme in the "Emperor" is a most majestic affair, and it would be the height of absurdity if it were to appear, *for the first time*, on the piano.

JOSEPH JOACHIM, 1831–1907
His cadenzas for many of the classical violin concertos remain unsurpassed
Oil painting by G. F. Watts, 1865. Watts Gallery, Compton, Guildford

Beethoven adopted a more conservative attitude towards the musical appendicitis known as the cadenza. In the first four of his piano concertos, and in the Violin Concerto, he followed established procedure—simply, one suspects, because that procedure suited the works in question. But in the "Emperor" Concerto even the cadenza is absorbed in the general design, so that at the twentieth bar of the passage the piano is joined by horns and strings, and fourteen bars later there commences a coda of revolutionary dimensions.

Beethoven's slow movements are highly independent structures, generally having little in common with those of Mozart, although occasionally the influence of Haydn may be noticed. In the C minor Concerto, Beethoven avoided the convention of writing his slow movement on the flat side of the main key, and turned instead to the brighter regions of E major. (In later years this practice was widely adopted by other composers; a popular instance is the opening of the Andante in Rachmaninov's Second Concerto, where the solemn orchestral chords are nothing more than a gradual modulation from C minor to E major.) A further instance of Beethoven's subtle key sense may be found in the "Emperor" Concerto, where the first note of the slow movement (D sharp) is simply an enharmonic change of the note with which the first movement (E flat) ended; thus, although there is a break between the movements, a subtle internal unity is achieved. Even more impressive, however, is the transition from the slow movement to the final rondo. At the end of the former the bassoons sustain the tonic note B, and one is tempted to assume that the movement is finished. But suddenly the note drops softly to B flat, whereupon the piano traces a slow, vague outline which lasts for two bars before breaking out as the exuberant theme of the finale. Subsequently, derivations of this device became extremely popular, but few composers have been able to exploit it with so powerful an effect as Beethoven; in fact, it is true to say that unless handled with discretion, and with a good musical reason, it becomes simply an irritating artificiality. In Beethoven's Fifth Concerto its purpose is twofold; the link serves as a dramatic introduction to the finale, and it brilliantly dispatches the music from B major to E flat without repeating the musical pun at the end of the first movement. A much more questionable instance is Mendelssohn's use of a similar link at the end of the first movement of his famous Violin Concerto.

The slow movement of Beethoven's Fourth Concerto is one of the most remarkable pieces of music ever written for solo instrument and orchestra. It derives, undoubtedly, from one type of Handel aria, in which the voice alternates with strongly contrasted orchestral passages. In the Andante of the Fourth Concerto Beethoven wrote a dialogue for piano and strings, the latter stating gruff phrases in octaves, and the former replying with restrained and tender expressions. The "conversational" nature of this music, and the fact that the two participants in the argument eventually blend in the most tranquil of agreements, has led many to the assumption that the music holds some discernible "meaning"; Liszt, in a legitimate analogy, compared the movement with the relation between Orpheus and the wild beasts. But whilst it is hardly a profound discovery to say that the music seems to indicate the relation between the arrogant and the passive, it is nonsensical to insist that it is illustrative of a specific, non-musical activity. In his *Lectures on Aesthetics* written in 1820, the philosopher G. W. F. Hegel, a contemporary of Beethoven, expressed the view that instrumental music amounted to little more than formal movement, whereas vocal music won its superiority because its meaning was discernible through the words. Yet in making such a statement he indicated no more than a profound misunderstanding of Mozart, Haydn, Beethoven and instrumental music in general. To deny any emotional expression to such music as the Andante of Beethoven's Fourth Concerto is no less absurd than to expect any emotional response it may cause to be precisely definable in words.

Beethoven invariably chose to conclude his concertos with a movement in rondo form. These rondos are often structures of some complexity, and the main themes undergo treatments sufficiently diverse to prevent the re-statements becoming monotonous. In that way Beethoven avoided the sectional effect characteristic of the bad rondo; the flexibility of his main themes causes the episodes based on them to be no less important than the alternating sections based on different themes. One exception to this might seem to be the Finale of the Violin Concerto in D major, where the simplicity of the main theme approaches the borders of triviality. In this case, however, the effect is probably caused by the remarkable emotional intensity of the first two movements, and in so far as Beethoven did not intend his Finale to be on so high a plane it is hardly his fault that some listeners do not survive the jolt.

The first movement of the Violin Concerto is endowed with a degree of spontaneous melodic invention that has no parallel elsewhere in Beethoven's music. Its exquisite lyricism at times diverts the conscious mind from its formal perfection, and there is nothing in Beethoven more beautiful than the G minor episode in the development section, nor is there another work in which all the musical elements are so symphonically integrated. The five drum-taps with which the Concerto opens amount to much more than a device for attracting the listener's attention; so powerful, in fact, is their influence throughout the first movement that sometimes they appear to have generated the rest of the material. The violin concerto is a musical form that reached maturity in Beethoven's hands, since previously it had been, with few exceptions, little more than a vehicle for virtuosity and technical exercise. In his D major Concerto Beethoven proved that executive brilliance is not incompatible with musical expression and logical structure.

Unfortunately, the same cannot be said of his Triple Concerto for piano, violin, 'cello and orchestra; the work is an interesting experiment, but the three soloists are not well accommodated in the structure, and musically the work is inferior Beethoven.

In conclusion, it is true to say that every innovation made by Beethoven in his concertos is capable of justification by a musical reason; the changes he made were invariably the result of deep thought, trial and experiment, failure and success. In the years after Beethoven's death in 1827 the concerto form became the object for even wider modifications, many of which derive directly from Beethoven. Yet an examination of the later romantic concertos in the light of Beethoven suggests that innovation and originality are not necessarily virtues, and can only be regarded as such when their presence is an internal or organic quality in the music. Beethoven's successors may have surpassed him in brilliance and effect, but none could equal him in power of mind.

LUDWIG VAN BEETHOVEN
Pen drawing by Moritz von Schwind

IV

THE ROMANTIC CONCERTO

BEETHOVEN'S conception of the piano concerto established a precedent that extended incalculable influence on the future of the form. The breadth of expression in the "Emperor" Concerto, and the equally important but subtler innovations of the Fourth, in G major, heralded the era of the romantic concerto, and also marked the advent of the virtuoso soloist. Yet the impact of his works extended beyond the period of Schumann, Chopin, Liszt and Tchaikovsky; the release of the soloist from the few remaining vestiges of *concertante* style was not simply a temporary matter, liable to be reversed in future generations. Except in certain isolated works, most of which are in any case not legitimate concertos, the soloist has maintained the individuality evolved through Mozart's concertos and brought to fruition by Beethoven. Yet the liberation of the soloist did not always result in something entirely satisfactory from the purely musical point of view; the advent of the virtuoso concerto, with its tendency to lay particular stress on technical display, resulted in a quantity of thoroughly insipid works whose small musical merits were buried beneath a welter of bravado. Most of these works, and the composers who wrote them, are now forgotten.

It was quite natural that the piano concerto should flourish as a form during the period in music known as the romantic. As we have seen, the concerto may in one way be regarded as a kind of musical representation of the relation between the individual and the mass, and although no composer wrote a work consciously to express such an idea, it is not surprising that this dramatic aspect appealed to the romantic composer. The extent of contrast in tone and volume between a piano and a symphony orchestra was capable of much development, particularly in view of the improvements effected in the pianoforte as a musical instrument. It is not within the scope of this book to attempt an outline of romantic principles and trends in music, but it is interesting to note that whereas the symphony declined during the period (compensated to some extent by the evolution of the symphonic poem), the concerto survived triumphantly.

One aspect of the mid-nineteenth-century concerto was foreshadowed by Weber (1786–1826), whose very effective *Concertstück* anticipated the Lisztian conception of a one-movement concerto, with the emphasis on display.

Mendelssohn's early works include two piano concertos—one in G minor and one in D minor—but both are overshadowed by his very important Violin Concerto in E minor. His piano concertos are interesting in so far as they are built on a small scale and yet display the characteristics of the romantic style; the G minor work is still to be heard occasionally, largely because of its attractive and neatly written piano part. The orchestral scoring suits the material, but lacks the grandeur and power of the fully developed romantic concerto. The Violin Concerto is a charming work of apparently unfailing popularity. Its fluent, lyrical style seems deliberately to avoid profundity, and its expert craftsmanship has made it the model of more than one later composer. There are passages of spontaneous counterpoint in the Finale so effective that Mendelssohn seems to have invented the two tunes simultaneously, instead of thinking them up separately and then fitting them together. And in the first movement he had the brilliant idea of placing the cadenza after the development instead of after the recapitulation, thereby delaying the return of the original themes and enhancing the movement with a particularly compact nature. Sibelius, who as a violinist in his youth used to play the Mendelssohn work, adopted a similar system in his D minor Violin Concerto.

A similar degree of lyricism is to be found in Schumann's A minor Piano Concerto—the romantic concerto *par excellence*. Schumann's inherent weakness in orchestration, although evident even in this work, is of little importance when one considers the luxurious blend of piano and orchestra achieved in the Concerto. The work has an interesting background. The first movement was written in 1841 (the year after Schumann's marriage to Clara Wieck), and was intended to be a Fantasia for piano and orchestra, complete in itself. Its composition coincided with one of the happiest periods in Schumann's career. Throughout 1839 he had suffered the strain of legal action through the attempt by Clara's father to prevent his daughter's marriage; Schumann's vindication after months of struggle and his marriage on September 12, 1840, inspired him to write a number of works almost all of which reflect the serenity of his life at that period; these works include the B flat and D minor Symphonies, the *Overture, Scherzo and Finale*, and the A minor Fantasia for piano and orchestra, which later became the first movement of the Piano Concerto.

The Intermezzo and Finale were added in 1845, and the fusion between these and the earlier movement would not be so remarkable were it not for the fact that in the intervening years Schumann suffered a serious nervous collapse—a grim indication of the mental disease which, ten years later,

FELIX MENDELSSOHN-BARTHOLDY
Lithograph, 1834

was to cause his death in Endenich asylum. In 1844 Clara Schumann took her husband to Dresden, where she hoped to restore normality to his tortured brain; the change of scene worked wonders, and the evidence is to be seen in the completion of the Piano Concerto, where the two additional movements are in such aesthetic and emotional communion with the first that there is no reflection of Schumann's intervening malady. Clara (who had herself once written a piano concerto in A minor) gave the first performance of her husband's work at the Leipzig Gewandhaus in January 1846, and since that date the Concerto has become a permanent and treasured item in the repertoire.

Schumann's Concerto retains certain features of the classical concerto, although like most of its romantic companions it dispenses with an orchestral exposition in the first movement. This movement (the original Fantasia) is perfectly constructed and exquisitely balanced, although any thematic analysis is bound to be rather complicated, since the bulk of the material is derived from one theme, played by the wood-wind at the opening of the

CLARA WIECK (LATER CLARA SCHUMANN)
Lithograph by F. Giere

Concerto and repeated by the piano. The balance of form is achieved not so much by the rhapsodical material as by the interplay of key, and it is along such lines that any worth-while analysis should proceed. But for the present purpose it is sufficient to draw attention to two particularly engaging sections of the movement. The first is the exquisite A flat major episode, in which the main theme adopts the character of a nocturne, the atmosphere of which is heightened by the unexpected modulation; the second is the cadenza, which is a perfect model of its kind: it gives the soloist ample opportunity for display but never degenerates into mere pyrotechnics, and its rhapsodical treatment of both the main theme and a fragment from a subsidiary idea constitutes piano music of the most entrancing quality.

The second and third movements—which, it will be remembered, were written some four years after the first—retain a similar emotional quality and also some thematic resemblance to the opening movement. The Intermezzo has a particularly lovely 'cello melody in its central section, and in the transition which leads to the Finale one can recognise the return of a familiar theme. The brilliant Finale is famous for its tantalising second subject, a syncopated theme in triple time, although giving the effect of duple rhythm.

ROBERT SCHUMANN
Lithograph after Adolph von Menzel

The fluency of the music is perhaps its strongest characteristic. There is hardly a moment when one feels that the composer's inspiration is slackening, or that the writing is no more than merely effective. The gorgeous pages of piano arpeggios and figurations in the finale are not simply externals for display: they are integral strands in a texture of romantic expression. It is impossible to convey in words the emotional effect of Schumann's Concerto, for that is something to be experienced by the individual. But it is my opinion that in this music Schumann touched emotional qualities never before or since expressed with such fluency, ease and charm. Others have undoubtedly penetrated the deeper regions of the mind; Schumann's work is that magical creation—a work of art that pleases immediately and retains its freshness despite repeated performances. It retires gracefully if one tries to analyse its emotional effect. You can profit in some ways by examining a rose through a microscope, but you cannot appreciate its complete beauty until you stand back and regard it as a whole.

If Schumann's natural genius for the piano was responsible for the perfection of his piano writing in the A minor Concerto, one might reasonably expect a similar degree of perfection in the concertos of Frédéric Chopin. It is true that from the soloist's point of view the concertos are admirable, and the piano writing—at once more florid and technically brilliant than that of Schumann—is indeed very beautiful. The same, unfortunately, cannot be said of the orchestration, which is perfunctory when it is not downright dull. Sometimes there is some confusion about the order of the concertos: the one now known as the Second, in F minor, was actually the first in order of composition, and second in order of publication. Both works were composed when Chopin was between nineteen and twenty-one.

Chopin's letters of this period reveal him as a youthful idealist, rather prone to violent infatuations. The slow movement of the F minor Concerto is an expression in music of his passion for Constantia Gladkowska, a pupil of the Warsaw Conservatoire whose voice he found "charmingly beautiful". Writing to a friend, he stated that "I have, perhaps to my misfortune, already found my ideal . . . Six months have elapsed and I have not yet exchanged a syllable with her of whom I dream every night. Whilst my thoughts were on her I composed the Adagio of my Concerto." But it is interesting to note that by 1836, when the work was first published, Constantia had faded from vision (she had actually married a merchant in 1832), and Chopin therefore dedicated the Concerto to a certain Countess Delphine Potocka. It was first performed by the composer at Warsaw on March 17, 1830, and it is amusing to note that the audience was not thought capable of enduring three concerto movements without some kind of intervening variety. This dubious intrusion was provided by a "Divertissement for French Horn", played after the Allegro. Later, when the remaining two movements of the Concerto had been played, Chopin received a considerable ovation.

The weaknesses of the concertos are to be found in the composer's attempt to reconcile his own style of romantic and rhapsodic expression with the elements of classical form (this becomes catastrophic in the first movement of the E minor work), and in his inability to write effectively for the orchestra. Attempts have been made to rewrite the orchestral parts of these concertos: Karl Klindworth re-scored the F minor work, and Tausig attempted a similar operation on the E minor concerto. But to-day, when the works are played, it is usually in the original version that they are to be heard. The excellence of the piano writing alone would justify occasional performances of these concertos, and the immense difficulties of the solo parts still constitute a challenge to the technique of any pianist.

Whereas Chopin's concertos are mechanically constructed on the bare bones of classical form, the concertos of Franz Liszt are both more adventurous and more rhapsodical than any of their romantic forerunners. In these works not only has the orchestral exposition vanished, but the three

FRÉDÉRIC CHOPIN
Pencil drawing by Rudolf Lehmann, 1847

movements have merged to make a continuous piece of music which nevertheless divides itself into sections that more or less correspond to the older system of separate movements. This continuity assists thematic economy, since the composer may use altered versions of one theme in each of the three or four sections. But Liszt was less concerned with developing a form than with writing effective virtuoso music, and in the latter respect he succeeded. His concertos, however, are rambling works singularly unable to keep to the musical point; they also suffer from a kind of musical malaria indicated by their tendency to break out in cadenzas at every possible opportunity.

The middle of the nineteenth century may be regarded as the opening of the virtuoso's golden age. Liszt and Chopin were the most important of the first romantic virtuoso-composers (Schumann, because of a self-imposed hand injury, cannot be claimed as a virtuoso), and they were followed by a long line of musicians, each of whom enjoyed a double fame as composer and executant. Among the more famous of these are Rubinstein, Medtner, Rachmaninov, Scriabin, Paderewski, Busoni, Prokofiev, Dohnányi

47

and Bartók. It is strange that all these should be pianists; among violinist-composers, only Sibelius in his younger days began what might have been a brilliant career as a virtuoso.

The style of writing apparent in the concertos of Liszt and Chopin epitomises the piano music of the period, and the rise of the professional solo artist encouraged composers to write music of extraordinary technical difficulty. With the demands of technique and effect in so commanding a position, it is not surprising that the finer elements of form, or the subtleties of suggestion as opposed to emphatic statement, should to some degree decline. To many listeners, there is more drama in the subdued opening of Mozart's C minor Concerto than in any Lisztian crescendo; to others, the physical excitement of watching a virtuoso battle through a full-scale romantic concerto makes earlier styles seem dull in comparison.

In any period of stylistic transition it is almost inevitable that there should be one figure determined to avoid the trends of current fashion while striving to maintain the ideals of the past. The creative artist who chooses so dangerous a path must be more than a talented imitator; to be successful, he must select from the past only those qualities that are essential to his own style, since without them his creative powers would be impaired. In the case of Johannes Brahms, one sees an extraordinary fusion of romantic expression and classical principles—a musician whose intensely logical mind could not accept the rhapsody, fantasia or quasi-concerto as a form for serious musical expression. Whether one likes or dislikes his music, it must be admitted that his motives were uncommonly sensible; he would have none of the mysticism with which his contemporaries liked to clothe the act of musical creation, and he regarded the "free form" of the Romantics as a creed more likely to encourage weakness than strength. Hence he remained unflinchingly faithful to the ideals of classicism, adapting the symphony, concerto, sonata and fugue to fit the demands of his own style.

The ideas for the First Pianoforte Concerto, in D minor, had been in Brahms's mind for many years before he thought of setting them down in the form of a symphony, which later he transformed into a sonata for two pianos. Finally, motivated to some extent by the death of Robert Schumann, Brahms again rewrote the music in the form of a piano concerto, which unfortunately was badly received at its first performance. The work has some imperfections, especially in the scoring, but is a courageous composition for a man of twenty-five, and it is not surprising that its austere and formal character did not find favour among audiences matured in the new romanticism. When the piano enters the first movement of this

48

concerto it does so with the utmost restraint, and it has waited nearly five minutes for the completion of the orchestral exposition; at the end of the Finale, it is the orchestra alone that concludes the work. Neither of these points is likely to have enthralled the mid-nineteenth-century audience.

The slow movement of the Concerto, because of an inscription in Latin on the score, is sometimes thought to be based on material from an early religious work that Brahms had abandoned; another interpretation maintains that the movement was composed in memory of Robert Schumann. The truth seems to embrace both these ideas, since it is clear that the music was drafted before Schumann's death, although the latter was the impetus that inspired the music in its present form. Whatever the case, it is powerful and yet poignant music, and its occasional use of dissonances (minor seconds abound in one phrase) indicates a strain of bitterness not greatly apparent elsewhere in Brahms. The Finale is a gigantic rondo which makes more than one bow to its equivalent in Beethoven's C minor Concerto. But it is not difficult to see why the work was for many years considered unrewarding from the pianist's point of view; the solo part, though extremely difficult, offers no opportunities to the pianist who wants to display technical tricks, since its demands are divided equally between brain and brawn.

The Second Piano Concerto, in B flat, is the emotional antithesis of its brother in D minor. Between 1878 and 1881 Brahms made two visits to Italy, and during those years he composed the new Concerto, which, to his friends, he described as "tiny". Yet what he had written was a work of enormous dimensions; the B flat Concerto not only comprises three movements of more than usual length, but includes an extra movement in the form of a Scherzo and Trio. This was a return to classical ideals with a vengeance, for although a four-movement concerto was an unusual departure, it is significant that in making his additional movement a Scherzo Brahms was in some degree restoring a symphonic character to the disintegrating concerto form. The soloist is permitted to enter before the exposition in the first movement, in a manner very similar to that of Beethoven's "Emperor" Concerto, but in no part of the work is any concession made to bravado. There are no display cadenzas, and in the serene Andante the main theme is the property of a solo 'cello, a fact which may tend to arouse pangs of jealousy in all but the most musical of pianists.

A tranquillity similar to that of the B flat Concerto is shared by the Violin Concerto in D major, a work of great beauty and perhaps the finest example of the fusion that Brahms achieved between classical form and romantic expression. From a pedantic point of view it would be possible to show that in structure the work owes a great deal to Beethoven. But this is a matter that lies more within the bounds of observation than criticism. The Concerto represents the synthesis of Brahms as a melodist, and there are few passages in his music more lyrically entrancing than the return of the main theme immediately after the cadenza in the first movement. The Finale is largely based on a theme that appears to be the ghost of some Hungarian folk tune, although it is a very jovial and Brahmsian ghost.

It may seem incongruous to conclude this chapter with a discussion of Brahms, since his music is not faithfully representative of its period. But his contribution to concerto literature, if not to concerto development, is of great value, and it is with music itself rather than musical development that most of us are concerned when we visit a concert hall. Brahms, however, had no successor; he was surrounded on one side by the nationalist composers who used traditional concerto structure with the utmost freedom, and on the other by those composers who accepted the mantle of the mid-nineteenth-century romantics, and whose works are more truly concertos by name than by nature.

FRANZ LISZT
Pencil sketch by John Doyle, 1840

V

NATIONAL IDIOMS

T HE development of distinctly national styles in concert music was widely apparent during the latter part of the nineteenth century. Audiences became aware of certain traits which occurred sufficiently often to be extracted from their contexts and regarded as "national" characteristics—an excursion from the particular to the general that did not always yield a satisfactory result. Bartók's researches into Hungarian music, for instance, have shown that the popular conception of Hungarian "flavour" is anything but authentic.

The concerto, being a dramatic and popular form, quickly adapted itself to absorb "national" idioms, and all the works mentioned in this chapter are coloured to some extent by their country of origin. Russian composers in particular produced a large amount of music that was strongly romantic in expression, pseudo-classical in form and plentifully spiced with national idioms. One of the works of this period—Tchaikovsky's B flat minor Piano Concerto—has lived to enjoy a phenomenal popularity, which to a great degree it deserves. Yet the odds have been heavily against this popularity; the Concerto's early history was turbulent, and the music has some intrinsic faults that demand strong virtues as counterweights. Were he alive to-day, the musician with the reddest face of all would be Nicholas Rubinstein (to whom Tchaikovsky intended to dedicate the Concerto), for in 1874 Rubinstein told the distressed composer that his Concerto was thoroughly bad and unplayable. There is some truth in the first of these observations, although the second is disproved at least twice a week in the capitals and larger provincial cities of England and America. (This instance is a clear indication that the technique of the virtuoso soloist to-day is more extensive than ever before. There is as much wisdom as wit in Arnold Schönberg's famous reply to the gentleman who told him that his Violin Concerto required a soloist with six fingers: "I can wait" was Schönberg's only comment.)

The most popular episode in Tchaikovsky's Concerto is paradoxically its strangest feature. This is the enormous introduction, which, apart from being in D flat instead of B flat, consists of a theme so powerful that it casts a very heavy shadow over the rest of the work. The first movement is, in fact, the most lopsided piece of music ever to gain a position in the

PETER ILYITCH TCHAIKOVSKY
Drawing by W. L. Bruckman

concert repertory, and it is ironic that most of the work's popularity is due to a piece of clumsy construction that has no precedent in the history of music. The D flat major tune with which the Concerto opens must be counted among the immortals, but what it has to do with the rest of the Concerto is an enigma that must remain unsolved. Such criticism is not a matter of pedantry, since any extended work must be expected to advance towards, rather than recede from, its climax, and even the tumultuous conclusion of Tchaikovsky's Finale cannot compete with the grandeur of the opening of the Concerto. (For an ingenious, but not wholly convincing, suggestion about this problem see Eric Blom's essay in the symposium *Tchaikovsky*, edited by Gerald Abraham.) Beyond this, the Concerto contains a great deal of attractive and effective music, and its form is conventional. The piano writing is hardly elegant or gracious, since Tchaikovsky preferred a heavy chordal style (with liberal doses of double octaves) to a more flowing arpeggio approach. But the style suits the music, and although Tchaikovsky's imitators seem to think it easy to write in such a style, their illusion is proved by their own weary products.

Tchaikovsky was unable to repeat the success of his First Concerto and neither the Second nor the incomplete Third can legitimately compete. The former has a tedious opening movement, a charming Andante in which the solo piano loses some limelight to a solo 'cello and solo violin, and a positively comical Finale that comes off brilliantly; the Third Concerto, in E flat, is in one movement, and adds little to what Tchaikovsky said in his earlier concertos.

Tchaikovsky was singularly unfortunate in the dedications he chose for his concertos; his single Violin Concerto suffered a similar fate to that of the First Piano Concerto, for when he took it to Leopold Auer he was again told that most of the work was vulgar and unplayable. Subsequently, the Concerto was first performed by Adolf Brodsky. Its first two movements are good, and each possesses considerable melodic fertility together with a degree of restraint unusual for Tchaikovsky; the soloist, however, receives ample compensation in the trite Finale, which consists largely of a wild and noisy Russian dance. As in nearly all his music, the demands of effect take precedence over everything else. The dramatic element inherent in concerto form had become melodramatic.

Apart from Tchaikovsky, Russian composers of the period did not greatly favour the concerto, although works were written by Rimsky-Korsakov and Scriabin. Tchaikovsky's real successor was Sergei Rachmaninov, whose Second Piano Concerto is now the most serious rival to the B flat minor. Rachmaninov, however, was much more than a second-rate Tchaikovsky; he was a phenomenally brilliant pianist, and as a composer for the piano he stands firmly in the tradition of Schumann, Chopin and Liszt. His four piano concertos, and the set of variations known as the *Rhapsody on a theme of Paganini* for piano and orchestra, together constitute the largest and most wholly successful addition to concerto literature made by any composer during this century, although they add nothing to the development of the form. The Second Concerto, in C minor, was written during Rachmaninov's recovery from a nervous breakdown for which he received hypnotic treatment from a Dr. Dahl, to whom the Concerto is dedicated. This routine case of hypnotic suggestion has been considerably over-dramatised by programme annotators, some of whom profess to find reflections of it in the music—a dangerous fantasy which approaches the province of Hollywood.

53

Rachmaninov's style, although deriving to some extent from Chopin and Liszt, is nevertheless strongly individual. The music reveals his profound understanding of the resources of the piano, and the solo part of his excellent Piano Concerto No. 3 in D minor is a model of effectiveness, fluency and economy. The latter qualities do not strictly apply to the music itself; Rachmaninov's music is at times extremely beautiful, although its range of expression is limited to the more sombre emotions. The second performance of the Third Piano Concerto, which took place in New York in 1909, was conducted by Gustav Mahler, who expressed great admiration for the work. The first performance, given some weeks earlier, was conducted by Waiter Damrosch, the composer appearing as soloist on both occasions.

Equally restricted, although in a different emotional plane, is Grieg's perennially popular A minor Concerto. Just as one may find Russian characteristics in Rachmaninov's music, so there exists in Grieg's Concerto a particular flavour which, if only through habit, we associate with Norway. Although superficially following traditional form, the Concerto relies mainly on the lyrical beauty of its themes and hardly at all on their development; yet the work extends a disarming freshness and charm, and in the hands of a sympathetic pianist its many fine qualities outshine its defects.

A national flavour is, in itself, a perfectly acceptable musical quality, provided that it retains its status as a flavour, and does not become the dominating characteristic of a symphonic work. An excellent example of a nationalist composer whose works retain firm principles of musical construction is Dvořák, whose 'Cello Concerto remains unsurpassed. The 'cello is not the most willing of solo instruments; its *cantabile* register is extremely beautiful but lacks power of penetration, thereby increasing the problems of balance in a concerto. Furthermore when given a short phrase or rapid succession of notes in the bass, it is liable to grunt. But in any case the 'cello concerto starts with a disadvantage, since the general music public prefers the more dramatic activities of a solo pianist to the apparent lethargy of a 'cellist, whose posture is liable to evoke impressions not entirely compatible with serious listening. Until Dvořák, the 'cello was something of a Cinderella among solo instruments; despite works by Haydn, Beethoven, Schumann and Brahms in which it played a solo part, its status as a soloist had not been firmly established. But in Dvořák's Concerto the 'cello comes into its own. The solo part is expertly written, and its music is entrancing. Dvořák had an unerring instrumental sense—an ability to choose the right instrument for his themes, which is evident in his choice of a solo horn, with wood-wind continuation, for the second subject of this Concerto. It is

RACHMANINOV'S PIANO CONCERTO NO. 3 IN D MINOR
A page from the autograph score

a tribute to Dvořák's insight, and to the lyrical powers of the 'cello, that the theme is no less beautiful when, later, it is adopted by the soloist. On hearing this Concerto, Brahms is said to have remarked that if he had known a 'cello concerto could sound so beautiful he would have attempted one long ago. He was not alone in his envy.

In general, as the strain of nationalism in music increased, the bonds of symphonic construction were relaxed, resulting in a number of works for solo instrument and orchestra that are not intended to be regarded as concertos. These will be discussed later; for the moment, it is only necessary to note that such works were partly responsible for the further reaction known as neo-classicism, in which certain composers of romantic tendency

IGNACY JAN PADEREWSKI, 1860–1941
The piano virtuoso who became the first Premier of the Polish Republic
Oil painting by Princess Louise, Duchess of Argyll, 1891
Polish Embassy, London

SERGEI RACHMANINOV
Drawing by Hilda Wiener from 'Pencil Portraits of Concert Celebrities', 1937

turned rather violently to ideals of classical perfection. Whether such a
rotation produces a satisfactory result depends more on the individual composer than on the ideal itself, as will be seen in the case of Saint-Saëns, an
eminently sincere French musician whose concertos display an alarming
disparity of style. The fluctuations between Bach and César Franck that open
his Second Piano Concerto are indications of a style, which, although
effective enough, never developed a consistent individuality. A finer blend
of neo-classicism and nationalism is to be found in the concertos of Sergei
Prokofiev; his Third Piano Concerto in C major is a scintillating work,
and is a synthesis of his strongly Russian melodic style, brilliant piano
writing and adapted classical form. There is no doubt that it takes a pianist

to write a really successful piano concerto, and in that respect Prokofiev, together with his more conventional compatriot Rachmaninov, descends from the royal line. His two Violin Concertos are brittle virtuoso works which seem to lack the substance and invention of the Piano Concertos.

Another work with its formal roots embedded in the past is the solitary Violin Concerto by Sibelius. Its relation to Mendelssohn's E minor work is similar to that between Brahms's First and Beethoven's Third Piano Concerto, although why this (together with the work's unabashed melodic appeal) should be thought a defect is a secret known only to certain of its critics. Apart from its structure, the work is consistently original, and its finale is as cold and bleak as parts of *Tapiola*; emotional contrast is, however, achieved through the warmth and passion of the slow movement, where effective interplay of soloist and orchestra is achieved despite an unusually extended melodic line.

If the origins of the Sibelius Concerto lie with Mendelssohn, those of Edward Elgar's inordinately beautiful work lie with Brahms. Elgar was the foremost British composer at the turn of the century, and his Violin Concerto was first performed by Kreisler in 1910. The score bears the enigmatic inscription "Here is enshrined the soul of . . .", and most of us would choose to fill the space with the composer's name. No other work, with the possible exception of the 'Cello Concerto written in 1924, provides so complete a picture of his style, nor so moving an indication of his humanity. It is a very long work, and it is far from being a display vehicle. There is only one cadenza, which is accompanied and appears at the end of the Finale; its purpose is to recall certain themes from the previous movements, and its hazy, nostalgic atmosphere suggests an altogether new function for the cadenza. In Elgar's treatment its display characteristics are sublimated in the interests of the most rarefied expression, and the passage—nearly seven minutes in duration—can be one of the most exquisite, or most interminable, episodes in music, depending on the soloist. The later 'Cello Concerto is in four short movements, and is structurally less ambitious than the work for the violin; again, at the end of the work, Elgar reverts to earlier themes, although in this case there is no suggestion of a cadenza: the music is a tranquil rhapsody, the musings of a great musician in the twilight of his career.

Among the remaining composers of the period who chose to write more or less within the bounds of concerto form, Nicolas Medtner, a Russian composer of German origin, wrote three attractive Piano Concertos which contain all the ingredients for a popularity they have never attained. In

SIR EDWARD ELGAR
Drawing by Sir William Rothenstein, 1919

France, Ravel wrote two concertos which refuse to be classified with any others, although both derive from romantic rather than classical models. The better of the two has its extremely exacting solo part written for the left hand alone, which is also the case in Prokofiev's Fourth Concerto. Although this feature might seem to strain the limits of virtuosity, Ravel's Concerto contains excellent music which would be no less excellent if the work had been written for the left foot.

The important developments in the concerto during this period have less to do with its form than with the type of sound that could be produced by an imaginative combination of solo instrument and orchestra, and in such a field experiments were carried out largely in works that are not strictly classifiable as concertos. The influence of these works on the concerto proper was evident when, in the nineteen-thirties, composers again began to write serious and original essays in the form.

VI

VOYAGES AND CONFLAGRATIONS

DESPITE the opportunities for rich and imaginative solo combinations—as in Bach's Second Brandenburg Concerto—the history of
the concerto is dominated by the two most satisfactory solo instruments, the piano and the violin. The piano provides the maximum
possible contrast with any orchestral group, and the violin, though considerably less powerful and lacking in qualities of contrast, is supreme in its
ability to sustain a long melodic line. Many concertos, however, have been
written for other solo instruments, ranging from Mozart's exquisite work
for flute and harp to Koussevitzky's Concerto for double-bass and orchestra,
both of which pose severe problems of balance. But Mozart, at least, could
never commit an infelicity in concerto form, even when writing for so
unlikely a soloist as the bassoon, while the superb music of his Clarinet
Concerto indicates the deep impression made by that instrument when
Mozart, as a young man, first heard it in Mannheim.

Curiosities abound in the history of the concerto. A number of these are
merely transcriptions, such as Beethoven's adaptation of his Violin Concerto
for the piano, whilst others are experiments in unusual combinations, such
as Maurer's Concerto for four violins and orchestra. Occasionally the use
of the title "concerto" seems to be based on the precedent of Bach's Italian
Concerto for clavier; this may be seen in such works as Liszt's *Concerto
Pathétique* (for two pianos) and Schumann's Sonata op. 14, originally called
a "concerto sans orchestre". Even less orthodox is Chausson's Concerto
for violin, piano and string quartet, and the limit of eccentricity seems to be
reached in an early Concerto by Arthur Bliss, which was originally scored for
piano, tenor voice, xylophone and strings. Yet all of these are works of
serious implication, which at once distinguishes them from certain less
reputable compositions; the lunatic fringe of concerto form had, in fact,
already been explored most thoroughly by certain of the lesser romantics.
Of these, the most outstanding was Daniel Steibelt, a contemporary of
Beethoven, whose grandiloquent ideas were hardly equalled by his musical
aptitude; his concertos, and their individual movements, rejoice in pictur-
esque titles such as "The Voyage to Mount St. Bernard", and the slow
movement of the Fifth Concerto is supposed to be based on a theme composed by Mary Stuart during her imprisonment. The Seventh Concerto,

PAGANINI IN LONDON
The violin virtuoso whose technique became legendary
Drawing by Daniel Maclise, c. 1831

being a "military" work, is appropriately scored for piano and two orchestras. Not to be outdone, other composers wrote works for the Panmelodikon and the Physharmonica, and even so fine a musician as John Field was capable of an occasional monstrosity such as his Fifth Concerto entitled "The Conflagration during the Storm", which uses a second piano to assist in the more literally thunderous passages. The minor composers of our time have shown less interest in such eccentricities, and it has been left to Hollywood to produce a concerto for typewriter. Needless to say, no acknowledgment was made to Erik Satie.

Such works as these, however, are merely reflective of a periodic trend in popular taste, and they are of amusement, rather than historical, interest. There are, however, a large number of serious works for solo instrument and orchestra which, although bearing little resemblance to the traditional concerto, nevertheless appear regularly in our concert halls and are generally classified as concertos. Some of these—and especially those which experiment with the tonal aspects of solo instrument and orchestra—have influenced later compositions in more symphonic form.

Liszt wrote a number of rhapsodical works for piano and orchestra, the most popular of which is the *Hungarian Fantasia*, an astoundingly dull work based on some of the material from his Hungarian Rhapsodies. His *Spanish Rhapsody* and *Totentanz* (both for piano and orchestra) are much more interesting.

César Franck composed two interesting works for piano and orchestra, one of which is a tone poem *Les Djinns* and the other a set of *Symphonic Variations*. The latter is an interesting hybrid, since it is neither a real concerto nor solely a set of variations; it consists of a theme and six variations enclosed in a network of symphonic development, and the whole is in one continuous movement which divides into sections roughly corresponding to those of the ordinary concerto.

Vincent d'Indy, a pupil of Franck, wrote a charming work for orchestra with piano *concertante* which he called a *Symphony on a French Mountain Song*. The work, which is in three movements, is ingeniously based on a simple, and rather insipid, folk melody, from which unpromising material d'Indy was able to evolve an attractive if not significant composition. In this work the piano is essentially a member of the orchestra, although its part in each movement is considerable. The difference in style between d'Indy's *Symphony* and the standard concerto is that in the former the piano is used for effect, but not virtuoso effect. A much more important instance of a *concertante* solo is to be found in Richard Strauss's *Don Quixote*, a tone poem in theme-and-variation form in which the leading characters are portrayed by means of a solo 'cello and solo viola.

At the turn of the century the rhapsodic work for solo and orchestra was greatly in favour; works such as Debussy's *Rhapsodie*, Fauré's *Ballade* and Richard Strauss's *Burleske* (all for piano and orchestra) are typical of the genre. In Hungary Dohnányi composed his delightful *Variations on a Nursery Theme*, solemnly dedicating the work to "the enjoyment of lovers of humour and to the annoyance of others". Its energetic and at times pointed humour together with its brilliant solo part has ensured the work

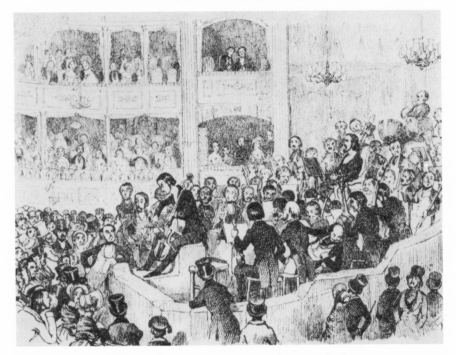

'GRAND CONCERT AT THE OPERA, NOV. 23, 1840'
Pencil drawing from Richard Doyle's MS. Diary

a regular place in the European concert repertoire. But none of these works could be said to point a new destiny for the concerto; most of them are period pieces, derived from the concerto but not substantially contributing to its history.

Nevertheless, one exceptional work did emerge from this somewhat mixed collection. In Spain, Manuel de Falla wrote his *Nights in the Gardens of Spain*, a quasi-impressionist work in which the piano combines the functions of soloist with those of assistant in the percussion department. Falla's use of the instrument in the latter capacity demanded a new modesty from the soloist, whose long reign of aristocracy was declining. Other composers showed an interest in the work; the effect, for instance, of a double glissando on the piano during an orchestral crescendo was a new kind of sound and seemed capable of further, if limited, application. In its restraint, and in its desire to create "atmosphere", the work has something in common with Vaughan Williams's *The Lark Ascending*, a pastoral episode for violin and orchestra which entirely abandons the virtuoso element and demands modest sensitivity from the soloist.

During this period composers tended to regard the piano as fundamentally a percussion instrument, which is its correct mechanical status. Yet percussive use of the piano was nothing new, since most serious compositions attempt, by such use, to compensate for the instrument's restricted powers of legato. The result, however, of too great a concentration on its percussive qualities was a series of melodically arid works, of which Stravinsky's *Capriccio* is a representative specimen. When, as was perhaps inevitable, this percussive ideal became wedded to jazz idioms the result was Gershwin's *Rhapsody in Blue* and his Piano Concerto, both of which display little beyond the composer's incredible but inherent crudity of style. They are now as dated as the aspidistra.

While these experiments continued, and while romanticism was having its last fling in the works of Busoni (whose Piano Concerto has a male voice choir in the Finale) and Rachmaninov, some of the composers mentioned in the last chapter were striving to revive the concerto as a serious symphonic form. Because of their work the concerto was able to survive through one of the most complex transitional periods in the history of music, but it was not until approximately the nineteen-thirties that the concerto again began to thrive as a stable form—a form that had changed greatly since the days of classicism or romanticism, but had preserved certain essential features that appealed to composers whose primary interest lay in symphonic music.

VII

THE PAST AND THE PRESENT

THE fluid and rather inconsistent character of the concerto during the last twenty years has led some to assume that the form is declining as a medium for serious musical thought. It is true that certain contemporary works seem to reflect little more than the death-spasms of the earlier percussive schools, whilst others return to the explosive lyricism of Tchaikovsky and Liszt. But it is still too early to examine the period in focus; when searching, in such circumstances, for the significant, one must be prepared to have the attention diverted by musical red herrings, and it is frequently the case that the latter achieve an ephemeral popularity denied to the former. Thus the concertos of Shostakovitch and Khachaturyan have won considerable popularity through their cleverly concocted mixture of earlier styles, flavoured with gentle harmonic spices. Khachaturyan's Piano Concerto in particular, if reduced to its essentials, is a series of episodes based on pseudo-Tchaikovsky and folk-music melodies; in the slow movement it emulates most of the later romantics by spoiling an attractive intimate theme through fortissimo repetition at the height of a thunderous climax, and in the Finale it pays homage to the percussive school and nods benignly in the direction of Gershwin. The inclusion of an occasional "wrong note" is sufficient to convince the more naïve listener that he is still in the twentieth century. His Violin Concerto, written in 1940, suffers from similar faults but is, on the whole, a more interesting work.

The revival of a symphonic approach to the concerto has been the prerogative of a handful of composers whose works have been received with enthusiasm by the musician, if not always by the public. The Violin Concerto by Ernest Bloch, for instance, is much more than an austere and refined reflection of the music in his better-known Hebrew Rhapsody *Schelomo* for 'cello and orchestra; it is an antidote for the type of musical mind that appears to deplore selection and symphonic thought. Yet despite its complex structure and considerable technical difficulties, the work shows that such characteristics are still compatible with deep emotional power, and that virtuosity may still be demanded without ugliness or triviality.

One of the most outstanding concertos of the century is also the most mysterious; it stands isolated, like a significant but distant landmark viewed from the main highway. The work is Alban Berg's Violin Concerto (1935), and as the composer was a disciple of Schönberg the ordinary listener may be tempted to classify his music as atonal, and therefore incomprehensible. But although the Concerto is based on atonal principles, the composer's emotional intensity breaks the bounds of that system and the result is a work of strange, remote beauty. The inclusion of diatonic themes (in one part a Bach chorale is quoted) is not an admission of atonal failure, but is an indication of the flexibility of that system in the hands of a composer who thinks musically rather than mathematically. The complexities of the score seem to melt in the warmth and serenity of performance, and the Concerto stands aloof from music of its own or any other period. Such sincere introspection is hardly likely to attract the populace, but its immortality seems assured.

Despite the profound impression made by Berg's Concerto on musicians throughout the world, it does not seem to have exerted much influence on other composers. The general trend of the concerto remained far from stable, although in England William Walton wrote two works that proved his complete mastery of the medium.

Walton's early *Sinfonia Concertante* for piano and orchestra is a brittle, flashy composition that is hardly worthy to stand beside his later concertos for viola and violin. The Concerto for viola and orchestra was written in 1929; it eschews romantic nationalism at one extreme and neo-classicism at the other, and is clearly the work of a composer whose motive power in composition is melody. A genuine melodic gift in any composer is discernible through the character and individuality of the themes which, whatever their tempo, bear certain features in common that impart a quickly recognisable quality. The presence of a distinctive style is much more likely to be found in a composer's melody than in his harmony and construction. The extraordinary angular beauty of Walton's themes is wholly original; he is a composer who has chosen not to abandon melody, but only to abandon melodic styles and cliches long since outworn; furthermore, he understands the use of extended melody within a symphonic framework, thereby giving unity and breadth to his music and avoiding the static repetition which is the last resort of composers who can create melody but cannot evolve it symphonically. The gradual expansion of the sixteen-bar melody which opens the Violin Concerto is a striking instance of Walton's ability to sustain the aesthetic quality of a theme that might at first seem incapable of further development. At the same time, the treatment evident in both works is essentially dramatic, since the soloist is always the dominating musical factor; the Violin Concerto in particular is virtuoso music *par excellence*, and it is

IGOR STRAVINSKY
Drawing by Pablo Picasso, 1920

significant that it is dedicated to Jascha Heifetz, who commissioned the work and gave the first performance on December 7, 1939. With the exception of works by Berg, Bartók and Bloch, Walton's concertos stand musically in advance of any others composed during the same period; they represent an oasis of sound construction and lyricism in a desert of rhapsodical pastiche.

All the significant works I have mentioned in this chapter were written for string instruments; the piano, although still the king of concerto instruments, was less fortunate. Among British composers, Arthur Bliss and John Ireland wrote piano concertos that are worthy additions to the repertoire. Ireland's work is a charming and unpretentious concerto that seems to lean rather strongly towards the models of Prokofiev and, strangely,

Ravel; the work has moments of considerable melodic beauty that compensate for some weaker passages in the Finale. It seems to be a common failing of British composers that the quality of their invention deteriorates as the tempo increases, since trivialities slip by more fluently in rapid and relatively noisy passages. The parts of Ireland's Concerto do not result in an altogether convincing whole, and a similar though lesser inconsistency is to be found in the Piano Concerto by Arthur Bliss. This enormous work was first performed by Solomon at the New York World's Fair in 1939. The first movement is formally the most classical structure since the parallel movement in Brahms's B flat Concerto, and the impassioned, relentless nature of the themes recalls the latter's earlier work in D minor. There is in fact a strong flavour of late romanticism in the Concerto, but the music is immensely powerful and virile. Even if it lacks a certain stylistic unity it does at least represent a return to a type of piano writing that uses all the resources of the instrument.

During the past twelve years British composers have signified a new interest in the concerto, and distinguished works have been written by Sir Arnold Bax, Alan Rawsthorne, Lennox Berkeley and E. J. Moeran. In particular, Moeran's restrained Violin Concerto seems likely to hold a place beside Delius's Concerto for the same instrument (with which it has something in common), and Rawsthorne's Piano Concerto is worthy of more attention than it has yet received. His later Violin Concerto is less convincing because of its loose construction and episodic progression, and the same might be said of the Piano Concerto and Two-Piano Concerto by Lennox Berkeley. The latter composer, however, shows a profound understanding of piano writing, and it seems likely that before long he may make an outstanding contribution to the history of the concerto.

A number of interesting works in concerto form have also been written by contemporary American composers; the largest and most significant contribution has come from Samuel Barber who, in addition to works for solo violin and solo 'cello, has written a brilliant concerto grosso for small orchestra known as the "Capricorn Concerto".

If this survey of the contemporary concerto had been written in 1939 instead of 1949 it might have had reason to conclude on a pessimistic note, since it could not have foreseen the remarkable series of works that were composed by Béla Bartók during the last years of his life. Three of Bartók's last major works are in concerto form, and together they seem to synthesise all that is valuable and permanent in the contemporary concerto; their originality, their return to an extensive use of melody and their balanced

PAU CASALS
The greatest 'cellist of our time
Drawing by Hilda Wiener from 'Pencil Portraits of Concert Celebrities', 1937

symphonic construction seem to herald a new era in the history of the form. Equally, they indicate the enormous scope that exists for imaginative scoring between solo instrument and orchestra; compare, for instance, the competent but wholly orthodox scoring of Arthur Bliss's Concerto with that of Bartók's Third Piano Concerto. The latter was Bartók's last composition; the concluding seventeen bars of the Finale existed only in draft at the time of the composer's death, and were subsequently scored by others. Some years earlier, Bartók experienced difficulties with the parallel passage in his Violin

69

Concerto, the score of which indicates an alternative ending; the opening, however, leaves us with no doubt that we are in the presence of a master:

The scope for new and imaginative instrumental treatments is further indicated by Bartók's *Concerto for Orchestra*, a huge contemporary concerto grosso in which a wealth of contrast is obtained between varied instrumental groups and between themes specifically allocated to the groups. The brass fugato in the first movement and the interplay between a flippant wood-wind theme and a dignified string melody in the fourth ("Interrupted Intermezzo") movement are but two instances of the composer's fertile imagination.

In conclusion it is possible to isolate three outstanding factors that seem to emerge from these compositions: a return to genuine melodic invention, a desire to evolve new types of tonal contrast between soloist and orchestra or within the orchestra itself, and, above all, a determination to write within a coherent and logical form. These things are fundamental in the concerto: without them no work has yet survived; without them there is no reason to believe that any contemporary work will live beyond its period. In the twilight of his career Bartók, while pointing to the future, indicated the essence of the past.

Yet there is an even deeper reason for believing that the concerto will not permanently decline. The contrasts and conflicts between the individual and the mass are an eternal human problem in life and art; they are epitomised in the spirit of a concerto which, whether it be by Mozart or Walton, is fundamentally the same. The musical journey from Viadana to Bartók is as turbulent and divergent as the history of man through the same period, but whereas our personal experience of the latter is limited to the part of it through which we have lived, our opportunities to explore the former are unbounded. Through the medium of words this book has made such an exploration; through the medium of music the listener may bring that exploration to life, for in the moment of musical performance the past and the present are one.

BÉLA BARTÓK
Sketch by George Buday, c. 1938

71

INDEX

(The figures in italics refer to the pages on which illustrations appear)